Fun Math in Everyday Life

Happy House

About Wise & Wide

- A systematic 6-level English reading program based on Lexile® measures
- Diverse and interesting topics chosen from the elementary curriculums of Korea and English speaking western countries
- Well-written books in various forms including fiction stories, descriptive texts, and classics retold
- The informative but original fiction stories grab your interest, leading to the easy and clear understanding of the educational content.
- Improve thinking skills with solid after-reading activities at all levels of the series.

Wise & Wide is a 6-level English reading program that consists of 60 books and each level is systematically divided by Lexile® measures. The Lexile® Framework for Reading is the most popular reading measuring system in American formal education curriculums and many English programs. Over 20 out of 50 states in the U.S. mark Lexile® measures directly on students' final report cards and over 300 well-known publishers adopt and use Lexile® measures.

Experience many kinds of readings written by professional writers from the U.S. and England. They used interesting topics that were carefully chosen after analyzing elementary curriculums from around the world including Korea, the U.S., England, and Australia among many others. Comprehensive after-reading activities including graphic organizers, speaking tasks, and After-reading Tests are ready for you.

Levels in the series and their corresponding Lexile® measures

Level	Lexile® measures	U.S. Grade
Level 1	Below 200L	Pre K - K
Level 2	190L - 400L	Lower Grade 1
Level 3	350L - 530L	Upper Grade 1
Level 4	420L - 650L	Grade 2
Level 5	520L - 940L	Grade 3 - 4
Level 6	830L - 1070L	Grade 5 - 6

* Smart Readers: Wise & Wide level 1 is applicable to the preschool level in the U.S.

* The source of the relationship between Lexile® measures and U.S. school grades: CCSS(Common Core State Standards) FOR ENGLISH LANGUAGE ARTS, APPENDIX A (2012, which is used by 45 states in the U.S.)

Topic List

Book	Level 1	Level 2	Level 3	Level 4	Level 5	Level 6
Book 1	Science>Biology: The hibernation of animals Story	Science>Biology: Living and nonliving things Story	Science>Biology> Animals & the Environment: Sea otters Story	Environment> Living with nature: The diver & the persimmon tree Story	Science>Biology> Animal: Amazing animals of the Amazon Story	Science>Biology: Germs, transmitted diseases Story
Book 2	Literature> World classics: Aesop's fables Story	Literature> Traditional fairy tale: Old tales about stones Story	Social Studies> Economy: To run a business to make and save money Story	Science>Biology> Plants: Photosynthesis Story	Science>Earth science: Earth's layers, earthquakes, volcanoes, and earth's atmosphere Report	Mathematics> Sequence: The golden ratio & the Fibonacci sequence Story
Book 3	Science>Physics: How shadows are formed Story	Literature> World classics: Peter Pan Story	Science>Scientific technology: Nanobots Story	Literature>Myths: World's creation stories Story	Literature> Legend: The story of King Arthur Story	Literature>Myths: Constellation myths Story
Book 4	Literature> Traditional literature: The Talmud Story	Science>Biology> Animal: Polar bears Story	Science>Biology> Animal: Mountain gorillas Story	Social Studies> Cultural anthropology: Amazing ancient cultures of the world Story	Science> Earth science: Clouds and weather Story	Literature> Human & animals: The friendship between a girl and a horse Story
Book 5	Social Studies> Ethics: Rules in daily life Story	Science>Biology: The five senses Report	Social Studies> Cultural anthropology: Astonishing festivals Report	Art>Music: Stories from two operas Story	Social Studies> World culture & history: The Renaissance Story	Sports> Board sports: Surfing & snowboarding Story
Book 6	Social Studies> World geography & travel: Tourist attractions around the world Story	Science>Biology> Animal: Dinosaurs Story	Science> Astronomy: The solar system Story	Social Studies> People: Three great people who overcame hardships Story	Science>Scientific technology: The wonderful world of robots Report	Art>Music: Composers of the Romantic Era Report
Book 7	Science> Space science: The life of astronauts Report	Social Studies> Cultural anthropology: Mythological monsters from around the world Report	Mathematics> Elementary mathematics: Numbers, measurement, shapes and data Report	Science & Social Studies> Technology & culture: Inventions from around the world Report	Art>Works of art: Famous paintings Report	Social Studies> Human & animals: Animals in action for human Report
Book 8	Social Studies> Cultural anthropology: Various living cultures of the world Story	Art>Music: Instruments in the orchestra Story	Social Studies> Life safety: Learning and using outdoor survival skills Story	Social Studies> History: The California Gold Rush Report	Social Studies & Science> Psychology: Psychology in everyday life Story	Literature> World classics: The Merchant of Venice Story
Book 9	Social Studies> Jobs: Interviews about jobs Report	Science>Scientific technology: Developments in technology in different times Story	Social Studies> Politics>Election: Running for 3rd grade class president Story	Literature> World classics: Stories of Sherlock Holmes Story	Literature> World classics: Adrift in the Pacific Story	
Book 10		Sports>Winter sports: Various aspects of some Winter Olympic sports Report				

* 10 books in each level will be published.

How to Use This Book

•Before Reading

You can easily find the topic and what kind of story you are about to read.

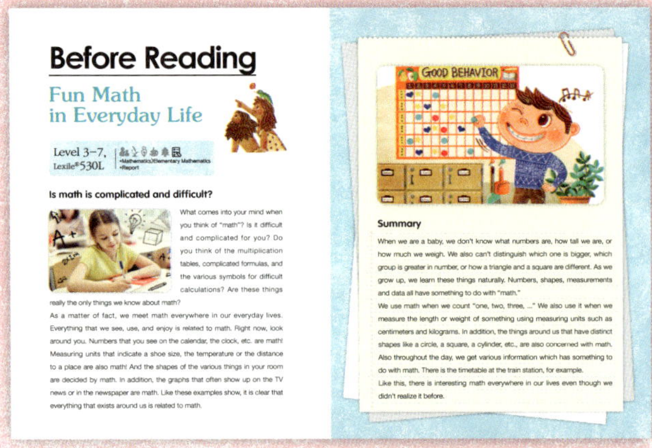

•The text

All the stories were written by professional writers from the U.S. and England, so you will read authentic and appropriate English sentences and expressions in every book in the series.

•Pop Quiz

Check out right away if you understand what you have just read by solving a pop quiz that checks your comprehension.

•Key Words

The key words and expressions on each page are listed for you to easily study them.

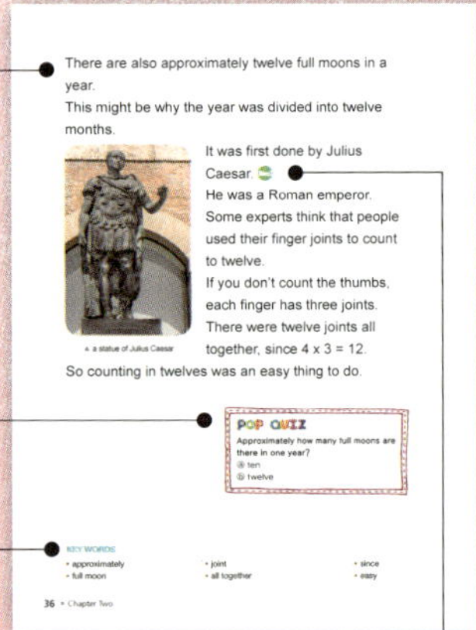

•Aha! Tips

Download free Korean explanations at *www.ihappyhouse.co.kr* for all of the sentences marked with "Aha!". These explain cultural, scientific, and economic knowledge or they deal with aspects of English such as grammatical structures or idiomatic expressions. There are lots of "Aha! Tips" to help you understand the text.

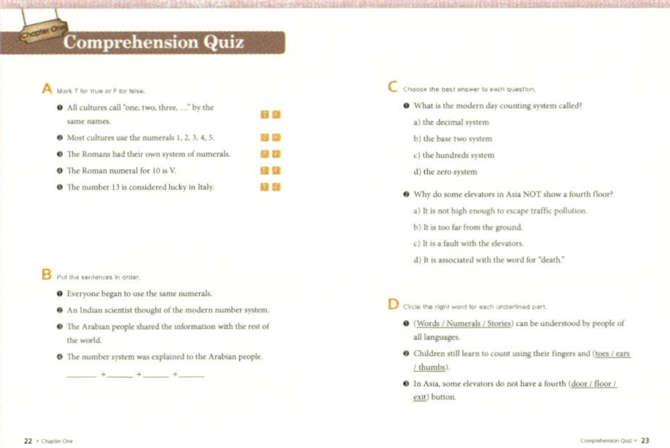

•Comprehension Quiz

After reading one chapter, solve various questions to find out if you fully understand the content.

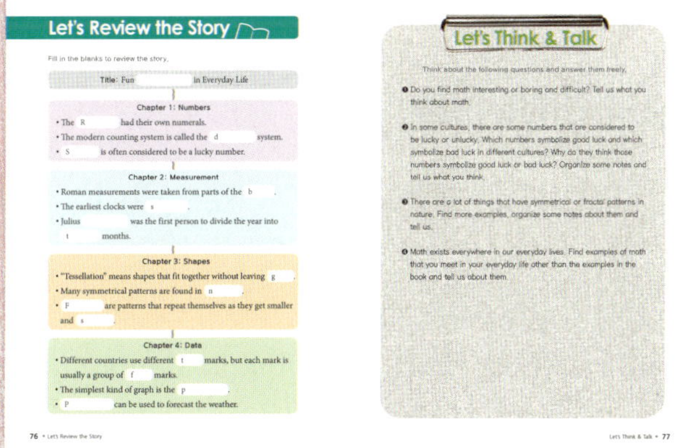

•Let's Review the Story /
•Let's Think & Talk

Fill in the blanks in the organizer to summarize the whole story. Express your own thinking and feelings about the story by answering the questions. You can build up logic and reasoning skills for your essay examinations in the future.

Appendix

Audio CD
In the CD audio book form, the texts are read vividly by American professional voice actors.
(MP3 files downloaded for free)

After-reading Test
Solve an additionally provided After-reading Test for each book.

The Korean translation, Answer Keys, a Word Quiz, a Word List, and Aha! Tips for each book
You can download them for free at *www.ihappyhouse.co.kr* or *www.darakwon.co.kr*

Before Reading

Fun Math in Everyday Life

Level 3–7,
Lexile® 530L

•Mathematics〉Elementary Mathematics
•Report

Is math is complicated and difficult?

What comes into your mind when you think of "math"? Is it difficult and complicated for you? Do you think of the multiplication tables, complicated formulas, and the various symbols for difficult calculations? Are these things really the only things we know about math?

As a matter of fact, we meet math everywhere in our everyday lives. Everything that we see, use, and enjoy is related to math. Right now, look around you. Numbers that you see on the calendar, the clock, etc. are math! Measuring units that indicate a shoe size, the temperature or the distance to a place are also math! And the shapes of the various things in your room are decided by math. In addition, the graphs that often show up on the TV news or in the newspaper are math. Like these examples show, it is clear that everything that exists around us is related to math.

Summary

When we are a baby, we don't know what numbers are, how tall we are, or how much we weigh. We also can't distinguish which one is bigger, which group is greater in number, or how a triangle and a square are different. As we grow up, we learn these things naturally. Numbers, shapes, measurements and data all have something to do with "math."

We use math when we count "one, two, three, ..." We also use it when we measure the length or weight of something using measuring units such as centimeters and kilograms. In addition, the things around us that have distinct shapes like a circle, a square, a cylinder, etc., are also concerned with math. Also throughout the day, we get various information which has something to do with math. There is the timetable at the train station, for example.

Like this, there is interesting math everywhere in our lives even though we didn't realize it before.

Contents

Fun Math in Everyday Life

Fun Math in Everyday Life

Numbers

When babies are born, math means nothing to them.

They don't know what time they wake up.

They don't know how much milk they drink.

They don't know how old they are.

They don't know when their birthdays are.

But you are not a baby any longer.

You know what time you go to bed.

You know when your birthday is.

You may know how tall you are.

You may know what your weight is.

So how did you learn these things?

KEY WORDS

- number
- be born
- **math** (= mathematics)
- **mean** (mean-meant-meant)
- nothing
- **know** (know-knew-known)
- what time
- **wake up** (wake-woke-woken)
- how much
- **drink** (drink-drank-drunk)

- how old
- birthday
- not ~ any longer
- **go to bed** (go-went-gone)
- may + *Verb*
- how tall
- weight
- so
- **learn** (learn-learned/learnt-learned/learnt)

Very young children cannot count.
But they soon learn basic math.
If you ask them to choose between one cookie and two cookies, they choose two.
Somehow, they know that two is greater than one.
People all over the world understand this.
Not all cultures have words for counting, but most do.
The words are different in every language.

KEY WORDS

- **cannot + *Verb*** (↔ can)
- **count** (*cf.* counting)
- **soon**
- **basic**
- **if**
- **choose** (choose-chose-chosen)
- **between A and B**
- **somehow**
- **greater**
- **than**
- **all over the world**
- **understand**
  (understand-understood-understood)
- **culture**
- **most**
- **different**
- **language**

"One, two, three" in English is "Un, deux, trois" in French.

Both English and French speakers may hold up three fingers.

They may count three cookies.

They both understand the *idea* of "three."

They just call it by a different name.

But most cultures use the symbols 1, 2, 3, 4, 5.

We call these "numerals."

They are like a sort of code.

They can be understood by people of all languages.

But how did numerals first begin?

Who invented them?

KEY WORDS

- French
- both
- speaker
- **hold up** (hold-held-held)
- idea
- just
- call
- name

- symbol
- numeral
- like
- a sort of
- code
- **begin** (begin-began-begun)
- invent

The Romans had their own system of numerals.

It is shown below.

Number	Roman numeral	Number	Roman numeral
1	I	6	VI
2	II	7	VII
3	III	8	VIII
4	IV	9	IX
5	V	10	X

There is a problem with the Roman system, though.

There is no symbol for "zero" in it!

They used the word "nulla" instead.

This made it very difficult to perform calculations. Aha!

So the modern day numerals were invented.

KEY WORDS

- Roman
- own
- system
- show
  (show-showed-showed/shown)

- below
- problem
- though
- nulla
- instead

- difficult
- perform
- calculation
- modern day (*cf.* day)

An Indian scientist first thought of the modern number system which uses 1, 2, 3, 4, etc.

He explained it to the Arabian people.

The Arabians then shared these numerals with the rest of the world.

KEY WORDS

- Indian
- scientist
- **think** (think-thought-thought)

- etc.
- explain
- **Arabian** (*cf.* Arabia)

- then
- share
- rest

Our counting system today is called the "decimal" system. **Aha!**

Sometimes it is known as the "base ten" system.
This means that everything is put into groups of ten.
This is useful because our fingers and thumbs add up to ten.
And children still learn to count using their fingers and thumbs.

We group things in tens, hundreds (10 x 10), and thousands (10 x 10 x 10).

The word "hundred" comes from the Old Norse word "hundrath."

Surprisingly, this means one hundred and twenty!

Many cultures used to count in groups of twelve (10 x 12 = 120).

Why was this?

We will look at this question in Chapter 2.

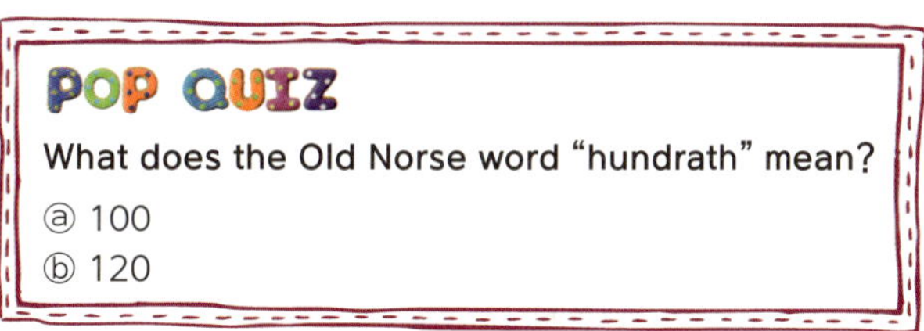

KEY WORDS

- be called
- decimal
- sometimes
- be[become] known as
- base
- put into (put-put-put)
- group

- useful
- because
- thumb
- add up to
- still
- hundred
- thousand

- come from
  (come-came-come)
- Old Norse
- surprisingly
- used to + *Verb*
- look at
- chapter

In different cultures, some numbers are considered lucky or unlucky.

In many Asian countries, the number four is considered unlucky.

In Chinese, the word for "four" sounds very similar to the word for "death."

Some elevators in Asia do not have a fourth floor button. Nobody wants to go there!

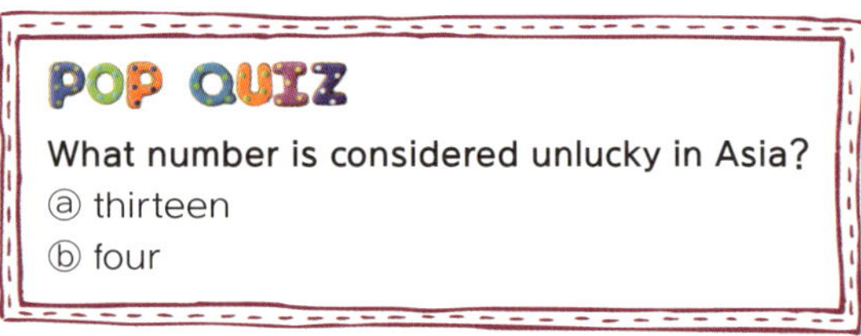

POP QUIZ

What number is considered unlucky in Asia?
ⓐ thirteen
ⓑ four

KEY WORDS

- be considered
- lucky (↔ unlucky)
- Asian
- country
- Chinese
- sound
- similar to
- death
- elevator
- fourth
- floor
- nobody

In most of Europe and the USA, the number thirteen is considered unlucky.

There are several possible reasons for this.

Some say that it comes from a story in the Bible.

At the Last Supper of Jesus Christ, there were thirteen people around the table. 

One of these people betrayed Jesus.

Soon afterward, he was killed.

▲ the painting of "the Last Supper"

KEY WORDS

- Europe
- several
- possible
- reason
- the Bible
- the Last Supper
- Jesus Christ
- table
- betray
- soon afterward
- kill

Others say that it began on Friday, October 13th, 1307. Aha!

On that day, the king of France killed a large number of knights.

He believed that they owned a lot of treasure.

He wanted it for himself.

Perhaps this is why Friday the 13th is considered a very unlucky day.

Some people are afraid of Friday the 13th.

They will not leave the house on that day.

KEY WORDS

- others
- a large number of
- knight
- believe
- a lot of
- treasure
- for oneself
- perhaps
- this is why
- be afraid of
- leave (leave-left-left)

Surprisingly, in Italy, 13 is considered a lucky number!

"To do thirteen" means to win the grand prize.

Seven is often considered a lucky number.

It is a number found in nature.

For example, there are seven colors in a rainbow.

In the Bible, the number seven represents the perfection of God.

There are seven days in a week.

There are seven wonders of the world.

People talk of "sailing the seven seas."

This means to travel across the whole world.

The number seven represents completeness.

▲ the Seven Wonders of the World
(from left. Taj Mahal, the Great Wall, Angkor Wat, the Colosseum,
the Leaning Tower of Pisa, Stonehenge, and the Great Pyramid of Giza)

KEY WORDS

- Italy
- win the grand prize (win-won-won)
- often
- find (find-found-found)
- for example (*cf.* example)
- represent
- perfection
- wonder
- talk of
- sailing
- the seven seas
- travel
- across the whole world
- completeness

Chapter One

Comprehension Quiz

A Mark T for true or F for false.

❶ All cultures call "one, two, three, …" by the same names.   T F

❷ Most cultures use the numerals 1, 2, 3, 4, 5.   T F

❸ The Romans had their own system of numerals.   T F

❹ The Roman numeral for 10 is V.   T F

❺ The number 13 is considered lucky in Italy.   T F

B Put the sentences in order.

❶ Everyone began to use the same numerals.

❷ An Indian scientist thought of the modern number system.

❸ The Arabian people shared the information with the rest of the world.

❹ The number system was explained to the Arabian people.

________ → ________ → ________ → ________

❶ What is the modern day counting system called?

a) the decimal system

b) the base two system

c) the hundreds system

d) the zero system

❷ Why do some elevators in Asia NOT show a fourth floor?

a) It is not high enough to escape traffic pollution.

b) It is too far from the ground.

c) It is a fault with the elevators.

d) It is associated with the word for "death."

D Circle the right word for each underlined part.

❶ (Words / Numerals / Stories) can be understood by people of all languages.

❷ Children still learn to count using their fingers and (toes / ears / thumbs).

❸ In Asia, some elevators do not have a fourth (door / floor / exit) button.

Measurement

Why do we need to measure things?

Measurements help us to share information.

Imagine someone says, "How far is it to London?"

You can tell them how many kilometers it is.

Imagine someone says, "What time shall I meet you?"

You can tell them to meet you in one hour.

Measurement helps us to organize our society.

The Romans used length measurements from parts of their bodies.

A "digitus" was the length of a finger.

An "uncia" was the length of a thumb.

A "foot" was… the length of a foot!

But there was a problem with this.

Each person's finger was a different size.

Each person's thumb was a different size.

So the Romans used the Emperor's measurements.

They used the length of his finger.

They used the length of his thumb.

Then, everyone used the same measurement.

Over the years, the uncia became known as the "inch." Inches were used to measure lengths in many western countries.

They also used feet and miles to measure longer distances.

Other countries used different measurements.

The Chinese "li" was the same as one third of an English mile. Aha!

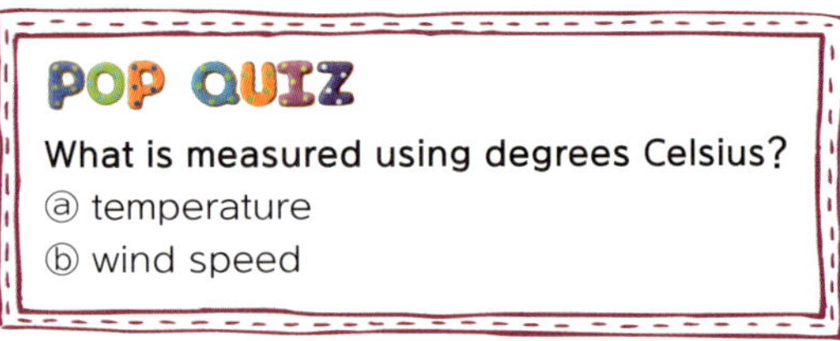

KEY WORDS

- over the years
- inch
- western
- also
- feet
- mile ($\fallingdotseq$ 1,609 km)
- longer
- distance
- other
- the same as
- third

In the 21st century, many countries use the
International System of Units.
In this system, length is measured in mm, cm, m, and
km. Aha!
Weight is measured in mg, g, and kg.
Temperature is measured in degrees Celsius.

KEY WORDS

- century
- International System of Units
  (*cf.* international / unit)

- temperature
- degree
- Celsius

Measuring length is quite simple.

We can see the length that we need to measure.

Measuring time is more difficult.

We cannot see time.

It has no beginning and no end.

We cannot pick it up and say, "Look, here are five minutes."

- quite
- more
- beginning (↔ end)
- pick up
- here
- minute (= 60 seconds)

The earliest humans did not have clocks. **Aha!**

But they knew that a period of daylight followed a period of darkness.

This was one day.

They also knew what time of day it was.

They knew it by the position of the sun in the sky.

KEY WORDS

- earliest
- human
- clock
- period
- daylight
- follow
- darkness
- position

The earliest clocks were sundials.

They can still be found in parks and gardens today.

As Earth spins, the sun seems to change its position in the sky.

Shadows get shorter and then longer as the day passes.

They change their position.

They move around roughly in a circle.

A sundial has a small piece called a "gnomon" that stands in the middle.

It makes a shadow when the sun shines on it.

We can tell the time by where the shadow falls.

POP QUIZ

What is the name of the small piece that stands up in the middle of a sundial?
ⓐ a hand
ⓑ a gnomon

KEY WORDS

- sundial
- as
- Earth
- spin (spin-spun-spun)
- seem to + *Verb*
- shadow
- get (get-got-gotten)
- shorter
- pass
- move around
- roughly
- in a circle
- piece
- gnomon
- stand (stand-stood-stood)
- in the middle
- shine (shine-shone-shone)
- fall (fall-fell-fallen)

The ancient Egyptians used sundials.

But they were only useful during daylight.

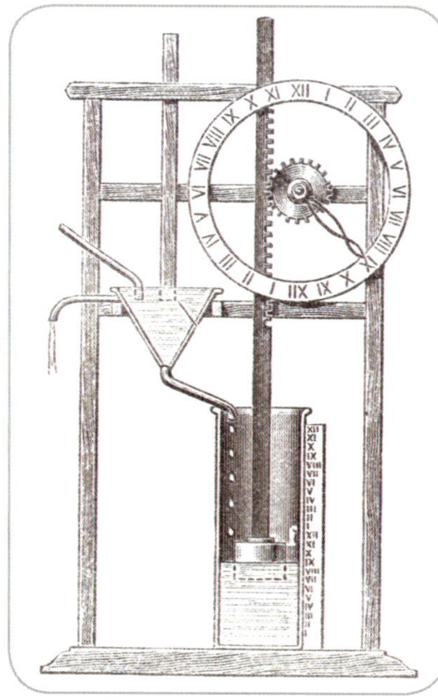

a picture of an Egyptian water clock

So they used "water clocks" too.

They were useful at night and during the day.

Water dripped into a container.

They looked at the amount of water collected.

This told them how much time had passed.

Other cultures used candles as clocks.

People looked at how much of the candle had burned down.

This told them how much time had passed.

KEY WORDS

- ancient
- Egyptian
- during
- too
- drip

- container
- amount
- collect
- candle
- **burn down** (burn-burned/burnt-burned/burnt)

In 14th century Europe, hourglasses were used.
These were made of glass and filled with sand.
The sand drained from the upper half to the lower half.
It drained through a small hole.

An hourglass with more sand or a smaller hole took longer to drain.
So there were different hourglasses for different time periods.

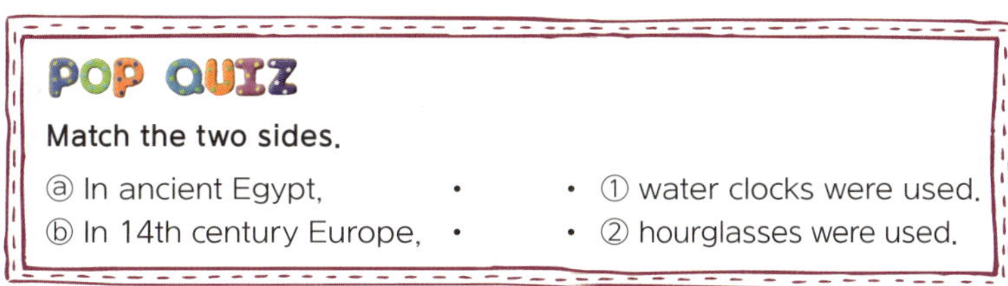

KEY WORDS

- hourglass
- be made of
- glass
- be filled with
- sand
- drain

- upper (↔ lower)
- half
- through
- smaller
- take (take took-taken)

Mechanical clocks began to appear in medieval times.
They were often displayed in town squares.
Everyone could see them there.
People did not have clocks in their own homes.
They relied on other people to tell them the time!
In England, watchmen called out every hour at night.
They told people what time it was.

Now, let's go back to that question from Chapter 1. Aha!

Why are there twelve months in a year?

Why is a clock face divided into twelve?

Experts have different ideas about this.

Some think that it began with the Babylonians.

They watched the constellations. Aha!

Constellations are patterns of stars in the sky.

They saw that different constellations appeared overhead at different times of the year.

They saw that there were twelve constellations.

They marked out the passing of a whole year.

▲ the 12 signs of the zodiac, a path that the sun passes by

KEY WORDS

- go back to
- clock face
- be divided into
- expert
- Babyloninan (*cf.* Babylonia)
- constellation
- pattern
- overhead
- mark out (*cf.* mark)

There are also approximately twelve full moons in a year.

This might be why the year was divided into twelve months.

▲ a statue of Julius Caesar

It was first done by Julius Caesar. **Aha!**

He was a Roman emperor.

Some experts think that people used their finger joints to count to twelve.

If you don't count the thumbs, each finger has three joints.

There were twelve joints all together, since 4 x 3 = 12.

So counting in twelves was an easy thing to do.

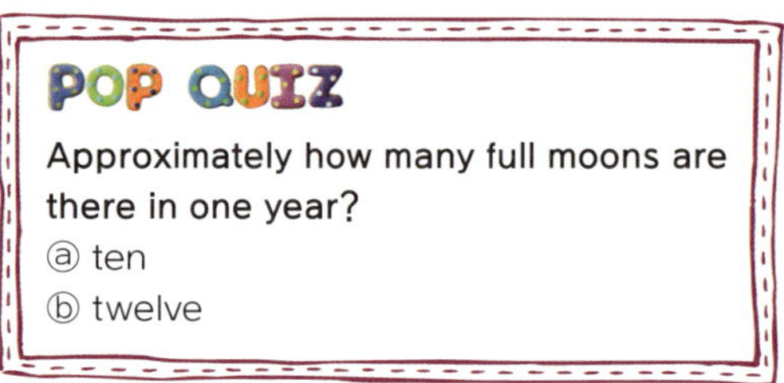

KEY WORDS

- approximately
- full moon
- joint
- all together
- since
- easy

Comprehension Quiz

A Mark T for true or F for false.

❶ The earliest humans did not have clocks.　　T　F

❷ The earliest clocks were water clocks.　　T　F

❸ Sundials work during the day and during the night.　　T　F

❹ Shadows get shorter and then longer as the day passes.　　T　F

❺ People counted in twelves using their finger joints.　　T　F

B Fill in each blank with the right word below.

used	passed	dripped	collected

❶ In water clocks, water ___________ into a container.

❷ People looked at the amount of water ___________.

❸ The water told people how much time had ___________.

❹ Other cultures ___________ candles as clocks.

C Choose the best answer to each question.

❶ How far was a Chinese "li"?

a) around one English mile

b) around one half of an English mile

c) around one third of an English mile

d) around one fourth of an English mile

❷ How did the earliest humans know what time of day it was?

a) They noticed that it got colder as the day ended.

b) They used firelight to make shadows.

c) They looked at the position of the sun in the sky.

d) They noticed whether the animals were awake or asleep.

❸ In medieval England, how did people know what time it was at night?

a) Everyone had clocks in their own homes.

b) They used candles to tell the time.

c) They got up and went to look at the clock in the town square.

d) Watchmen called out the time every hour.

Shapes

Math is not only about numbers.

Shapes are part of math, too. Aha!

Shapes are all around us.

Stop reading for a moment and look around you.

How many different shapes can you see?

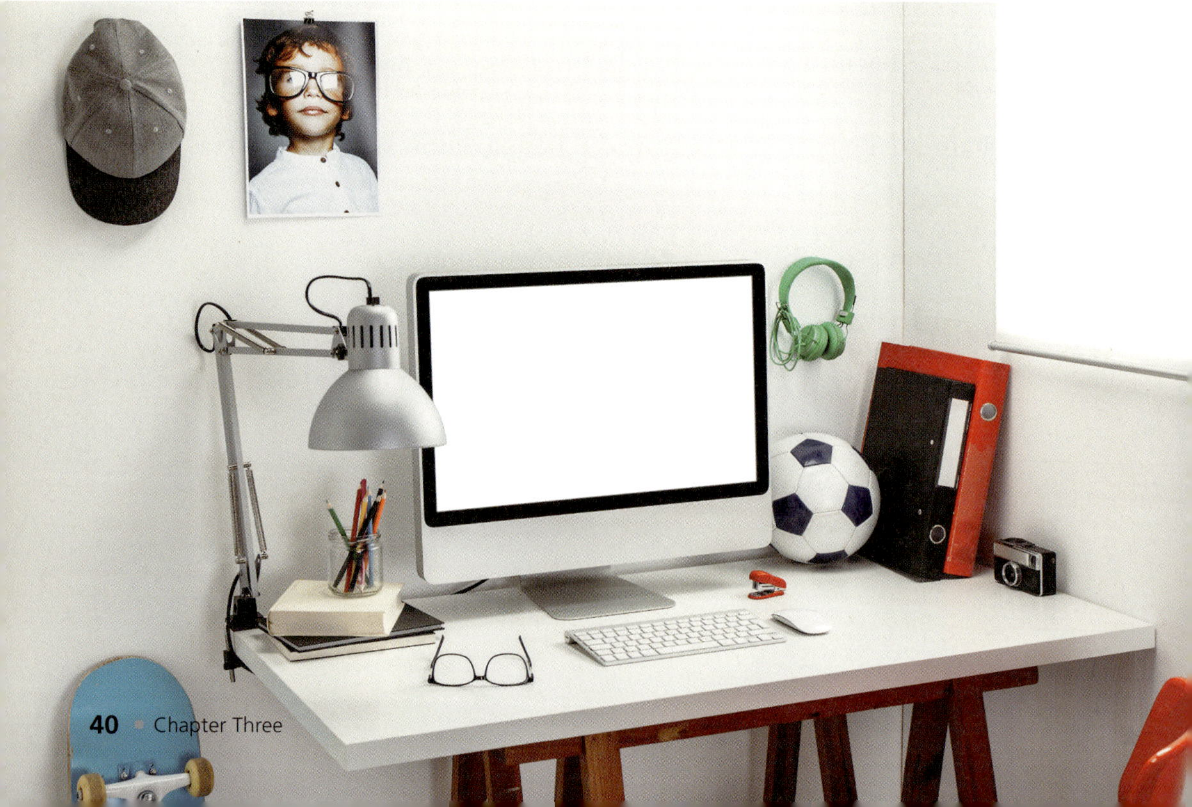

Have you ever thought about *why* things are a particular shape?

The book that you are holding is a rectangle.

Why isn't it a circle?

If it was a circle, it would be difficult to store on a shelf. It would roll off!

Why isn't it a triangle?

If it was a triangle, not as many words would fit on each page.

When humans design things, they must think about the shape.

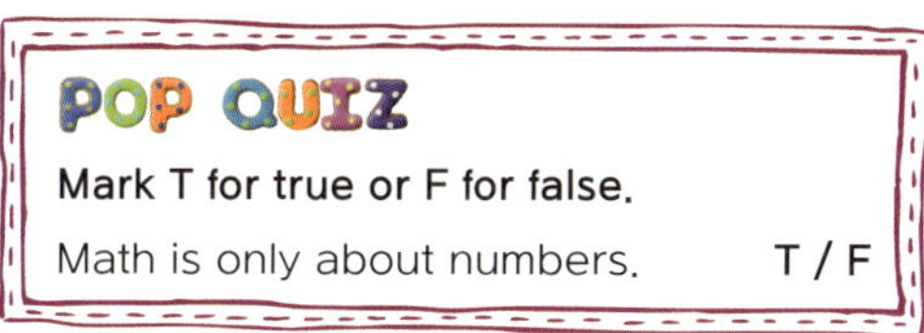

KEY WORDS

- for a moment
- look around
- have ever + *p.p.*
- particular
- rectangle

- circle
- store
- shelf
- roll off
- triangle

- as many
- **fit** (fit-fit-fit)
- page
- design
- must + *Verb*

Floor or wall tiles must fit together.

There must not be any gaps between them.

If there were gaps, dirt would collect there.

This is called "tessellation."

Shapes that tessellate fit together without any gaps.

Squares and rectangles are most often used for tiles.

They fit together easily.

But some surprising shapes can be used.

Tables can be squares, rectangles, or circles.

Sometimes, people choose a square or rectangular table for their home.

It fits easily into a square or rectangular room.

But some people choose a circle.

More people can sit comfortably around a circular table.

Nobody has to sit at a corner!

KEY WORDS

- wall
- tile
- fit together
- gap
- dirt
- tessellation
- tessellate

- without
- easily
- surprising
- **sit** (sit-sat-sat)
- comfortably
- **have to + *Verb*** (have-had-had)
- **at a corner** (*cf.* corner)

Have you ever wondered why food cans are usually cylinders?

There are several reasons for this.

Food manufacturers put food into the cans.

They want to fit in as much food as possible.

A cylinder holds more food than a cuboid of the same size.

A sphere holds even more than a cylinder.

But a sphere would roll off the shelf.

They would roll off the shelf and fall onto the floor.

▲ cylinder   ▲ cuboid   ▲ sphere

KEY WORDS

- usually
- cylinder
- manufacturer
- put
- as ~ as possible
- cuboid
- sphere
- even

A cylinder is better than a cuboid for another reason.

A cylinder has smooth edges.

There are no sharp corners to hurt yourself on.

It is also easier to scrape food out of a cylinder.

There are no corners for the food
to get stuck in. Aha!

It will still sit safely on a shelf
without falling off.

Cylinders can also be stacked on
top of each other.

KEY WORDS

- better
- another
- smooth
- edge
- sharp

- hurt oneself (hurt-hurt-hurt)
- easier
- scrape
- out of
- get stuck

- safely
- be stacked
- each other

Many different shapes are found in nature.

Cut an okra plant across the stem.

You will see that it is a pentagon shape.

Look at honeycomb cells from a beehive.

They are perfect hexagons.

Many natural shapes are symmetrical.

This means that a pattern or shape is the same on both sides.

▲ okra

▲ honeycomb cells

KEY WORDS

- okra
- plant
- across
- stem

- pentagon
- honeycomb
- cell
- beehive

- perfect
- hexagon
- natural
- symmetrical

The tail of a peacock is symmetrical.

Both the left and right sides of the tail are exactly the same.

This helps peacocks to attract females.

Females believe that symmetrical males are healthier.

They want to mate with them and have babies.

- tail
- peacock
- exactly
- attract
- female
- male
- healthier
- mate
- have a baby

There are also many other examples of symmetry in
the animal world;
Butterflies have symmetrical patterns on their wings.
Ladybugs have symmetrical spot patterns.

Most human faces are roughly symmetrical, too.
The human face has an eye on each side.
It has a nose and a mouth in the middle.
But few human faces are completely symmetrical.

Most of us have one eyebrow higher than the other.

Or perhaps we have a mouth that turns up at one side.

Scientists have studied human faces.

They believe that people with more symmetrical faces are more attractive.  But some people find symmetrical faces boring to look at. They think that a face which is not symmetrical is more interesting.

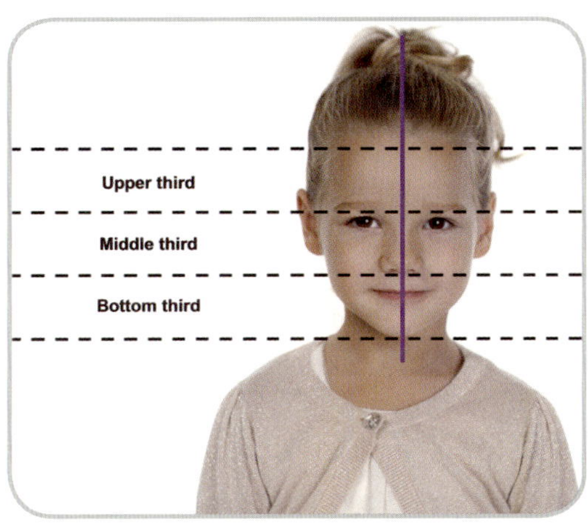

▲ an example of a symmetrical face

POP QUIZ

Mark T for true or F for false.

Scientists believe that people with more symmetrical faces are more attractive.   T / F

- eyebrow
- higher
- the other

- turn up
- attractive
- boring

- interesting

Some animals are even symmetrical on the inside!

Frogs are exactly the same on both sides.

Humans are not symmetrical on the inside.

The heart is toward the left side of the body.

Other organs are on the right or the left.

Snowflakes are symmetrical.

Even in space, our own galaxy, the Milky Way, is symmetrical. 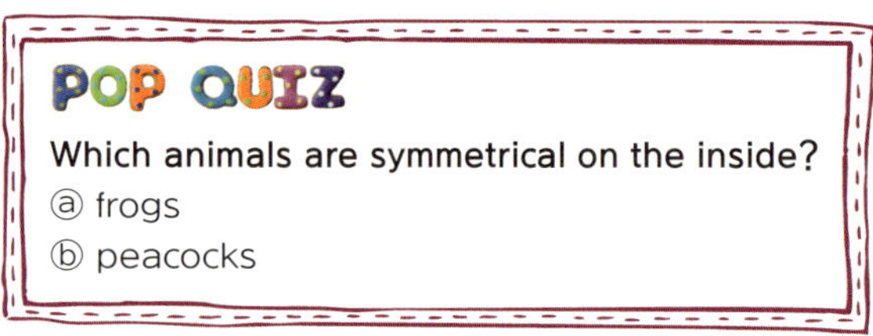

Scientists recently discovered a new section of the galaxy.

They discovered that it is almost perfectly symmetrical.

POP QUIZ

Which animals are symmetrical on the inside?
ⓐ frogs
ⓑ peacocks

KEY WORDS

- on the inside
- frog
- heart
- toward
- organ

- snowflake
- space
- galaxy
- the Milky Way
- recently

- discover
- section
- almost
- perfectly

▲ a frog dissection diagram

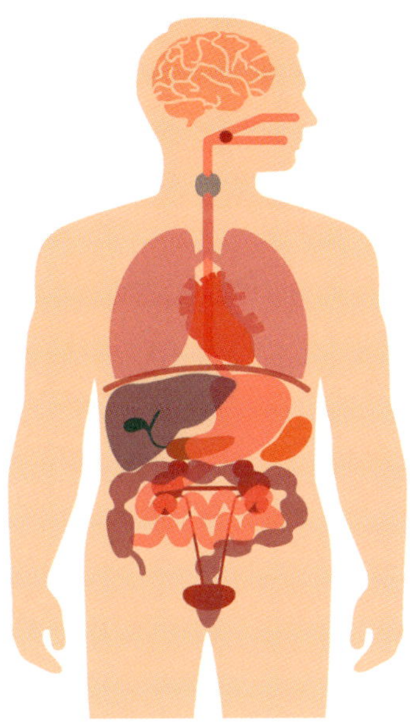

▲ a human internal organ diagram

▲ a magnified snowflake

▲ the Milky Way

Fractals are a fascinating part of nature.

Fractals are never-ending patterns.

They repeat themselves as they get smaller and smaller.

The leaves of ferns are a good example.

Look at this picture closely.

Look at the small leaflets along the stem.

Each one looks exactly like the big leaf.

Look more closely still.

Each part of the small leaflets is made of even smaller ones.

They are also exactly the same!

Fractals can also occur on a much larger scale.

Rivers carve out valleys over thousands of years.

They branch and then branch again.

This forms a fractal pattern.

Lightning makes a fractal pattern, too.

It forks in two, and each fork splits again.

KEY WORDS

- leaflet
- along
- occur
- larger
- scale

- carve out
- valley
- over
- thousands of years
- branch

- form
- lightning
- fork
- split

Chapter Three

Comprehension Quiz

A Choose the best answer to each question.

❶ Why is it important for tiles to fit together without gaps?

a) If there were gaps, the pattern would look untidy.

b) If there were gaps, dirt would collect in them.

c) If there were gaps, people might trip over them.

d) If there were gaps, the tiles would come loose.

❷ What did scientists recently discover about the Milky Way?

a) It contains more planets than they thought.

b) It is shaped like a snowflake.

c) It is almost perfectly symmetrical.

d) There is life on some of the planets there.

B Mark T for true or F for false.

❶ A cylinder has no sharp corners. ⬛T ⬛F

❷ It is easier to scrape food out of a cuboid than a cylinder. ⬛T ⬛F

❸ A cylinder will sit safely on a shelf without falling off. ⬛T ⬛F

C Solve the crossword puzzle.

❷ The Milky Way is a g__________.

❸ A shape that can t__________ will fit together without any gaps.

❺ A never-ending pattern that repeats itself is called a f__________.

❶ Patterns that are the same on both sides are s__________.

❹ A peacock's t__________ is designed to attract a female.

Data

What *are* data?

You might think that the question is incorrect.

You might think that it should say, "What *is* data?"

But "data" is a plural word.

It means different pieces of information gathered together.

A single piece of information is called a "datum."

Data are used to gain information.

They are used to make decisions.

They are even used to predict the future!

Data are often presented as pictures, graphs, or numbers. This is quicker and easier than writing information down. People who speak

different languages can understand the data. Aha!

Everyone can understand numbers and pictures.

KEY WORDS

- **incorrect** ($\leftrightarrow$ correct)
- **should** + *Verb*
- **plural**
- **gather**
- **single**
- **datum**
- **gain**

- **make a decision** (make-made-made)
- **predict**
- **future**
- **present**
- **graph**
- **quicker**
- **write down** (write-wrote-written)

Also, a lot of information can be shown in a small space.

Think about a train timetable.

Destination	Platform	Departure Time
London	4	3:15

A train is traveling to London. Aha!

It leaves from Platform Four.

It leaves at fifteen minutes past three. Aha!

It takes a lot of space to write this down!

It is easier to put the information in a table.

One way to keep a record of data is by a tally.

This is an old way of recording data.

It has been used for hundreds of years.

A tally is a group of marks.

Each tally represents one item or object.

The marks are grouped in fives.

It is easy for people to count in fives.

The simplest tally for the numbers 1~5 looks like this.

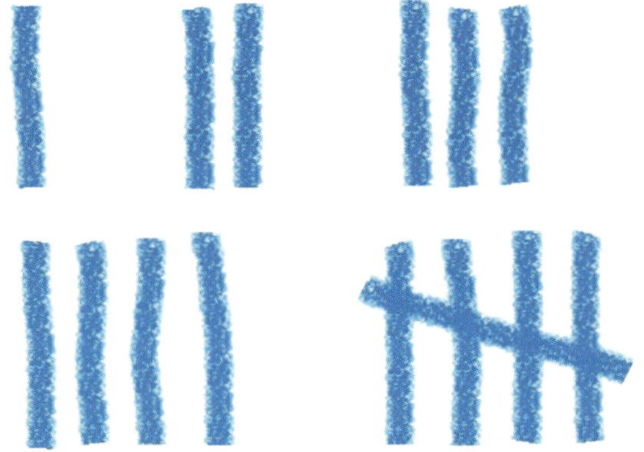

KEY WORDS

- keep a record
  (keep-kept-kept)(*cf.* record)
- tally
- hundreds of years
- item
- object
- simplest
- look like

This method is useful if data change from day to day.
Prisoners in jail used to scratch tally marks on the wall.
They added one mark each day.
The marks showed how many days had passed.

People in many French and Spanish-speaking
countries use a different tally mark.
They still add one straight line each time.
They still make groups of five lines.

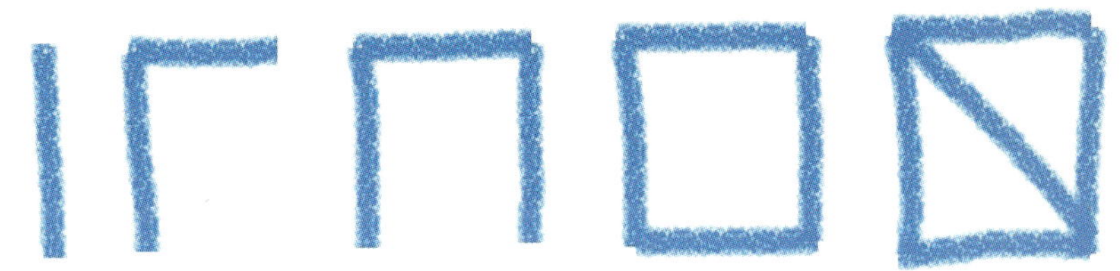

In Asia, yet another tally mark is used.
It is still based on groups of five lines.

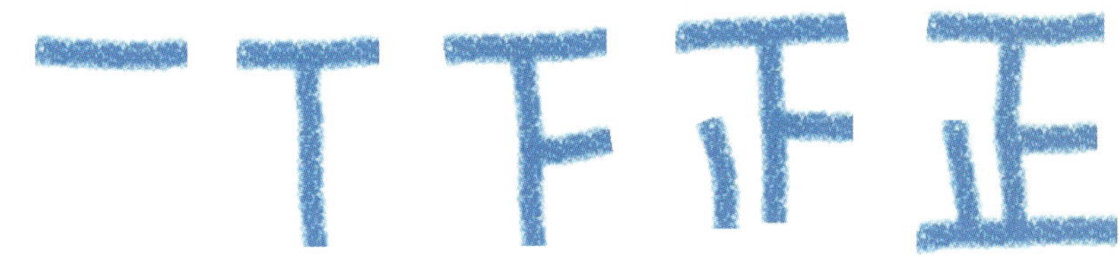

- method
- from day to day
- prisoner
- jail
- scratch

- add
- each day
- French
- Spanish
- straight line

- each time
- Asia
- yet
- be based on

Graphs are a good way to present data.

People can look at a graph and understand it at once.

The simplest graph is the pictograph.

This shows actual pictures of things.

A good example is a sticker chart.

It might be displayed in a school classroom.

When children behave well, they receive a sticker.

They put a sticker on the chart next to their name.

They can see at once who has got the most stickers.

They know who behaved well.

Another kind of graph or chart is the "pie chart."

It is called this because it looks like a pie.

In France, it is called a "camembert."

A camembert is a large, round, French cheese!

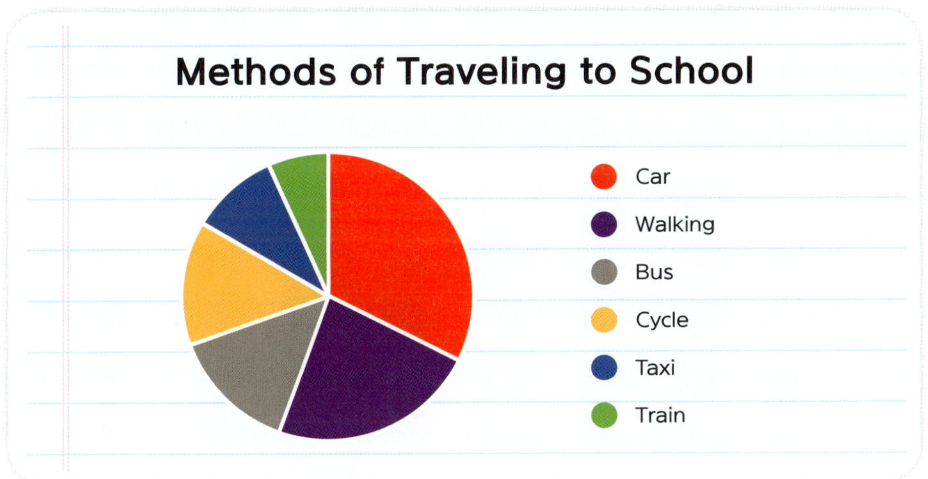

In this pie chart, the biggest piece of "pie" is the red one.

This tells us that most children at this school travel there by car.

KEY WORDS

- at once
- pictograph
- actual
- sticker
- chart
- classroom
- behave well
- receive
- next to
- kind
- pie chart (*cf.* pie)
- France
- camembert
- biggest
- by car (*cf.* by)

Some graphs show data as bars of information.
This graph is about ice cream sales.
It shows how many were sold on each day of the week.

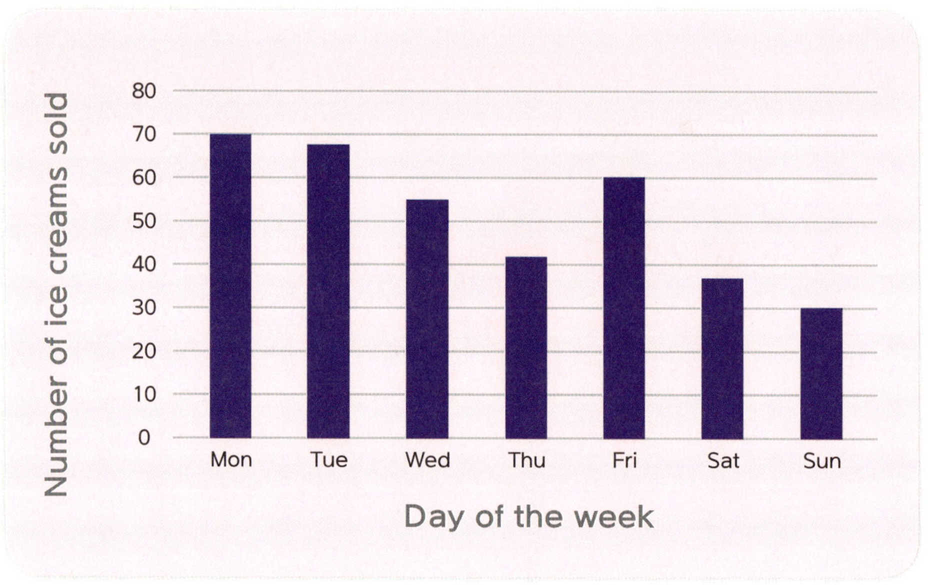

Ice cream sellers can use this information.
It can help them in their work.
They look at the data.
They see that most ice creams were sold on Monday and Tuesday.
So they make sure that they have extra ice creams for those days.
They are ready to sell more on Mondays and Tuesdays.

Data can help us to make decisions.

Parents expecting a baby can look at data.

They can look at lists of popular baby names.

These can be found on websites.

Sometimes the lists are published in the newspaper.

English and American parents may choose a name this way.

They might choose a popular one.

They might choose one that nobody else has chosen.

KEY WORDS

- bar
- sale
- **sell** (sell-sold-sold)
- day of the week
- seller
- make sure

- extra
- be ready to + *Verb*
- parent
- expect a baby
- list
- popular

- website
- publish
- newspaper
- nobody else

Even the words "yes" and "no" are data.

They can be used in a flow diagram.

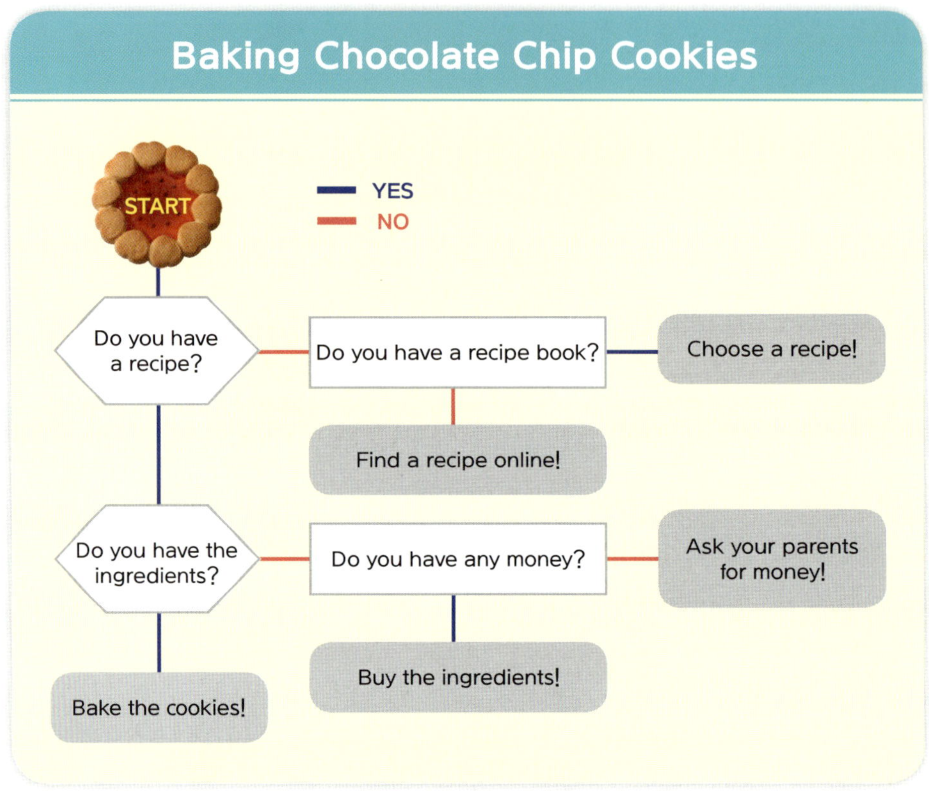

▲ an example of a flow diagram

Data can be used to predict the future.

This is called probability.

Some things are certain to happen.

The probability is 100%.

It is 100% likely that the sun will rise tomorrow morning!

Some things are certain *not* to happen. 

The probability is 0%.

It is 0% likely that you will be younger next year than you are now!

Probability is calculated by looking at data.

The data tells us about what has happened in the past.

Then, we can apply it to the future.

KEY WORDS

- probability
- be certain to + *Verb*
- happen
- it is likely that (*cf.* likely)
- rise (rise-rose-risen)
- younger
- calculate
- in the past
- apply

Probability is used to forecast the weather.

Weather experts look at weather data.

They look at temperature data.

They look at wind speed data.

They look at rainfall and sunshine data.

They measure how much water is in a cloud.

They measure how cold the air is within the cloud.

They measure how quickly the cloud is moving.

Then, they predict when the cloud will reach land.

They predict how much water it will hold.

In this way, they can calculate the probability that rain will fall on a particular city.

They may say that there is a 50% probability of rain at a particular time.

They do not know for sure what will happen.

But they can tell people how likely it is to happen.

Then, it is up to the people of that city to think for themselves.

They decide whether to carry umbrellas when they go out!

KEY WORDS

- forecast
- weather
- wind speed
- rainfall
- sunshine
- within
- reach
- for sure
- be up to
- decide
- whether
- carry
- umbrella
- go out

Sometimes, people use probability to make money.

Some people gamble on the outcome of sporting events.

This means that they pay some of their own money for the chance of winning more money.

Some people gamble on horse races.

They look at data about how many races each horse has won.

They look at data about the weather.

They look at data about how hard or soft the race track is.

They use these data to make calculations.

They calculate the probability that each horse will win.

Then, they choose which horse to gamble on.

POP QUIZ

Mark T for true or F for false.

Many people may lose a lot of money by gambling on sporting events.   T / F

Very few people make a lot of money this way.

But many people lose a lot of money.

It is very risky.

They can never be certain that their horse will win.

Gambling in this way is very dangerous.

- **lose** (lose-lost-lost)
- **risky**
- **never**
- **gambling**
- **dangerous**

But many people gamble in a much safer way. Aha!

They buy a lottery ticket.

They guess which numbers will be chosen that week.

They pay a very small amount of money to take part.

So they don't lose a lot of money.

Most people win nothing.

But sometimes, they win large amounts of money!

KEY WORDS

- safer
- buy
  (buy-bought-bought)
- lottery ticket
- guess
- take part
- all around
- beauty

Math is all around us.

We see it in nature.

We see it in human design.

We see it at school and at home.

Take some time to look.

Discover the beauty of math.

You will never look at the world the same way again!

Comprehension Quiz

A Fill in each blank with the right word below.

measure	happen	forecast	certain

❶ Probability is used to ___________ the weather.

❷ Some things are certain not to __________. The probability is 0%.

❸ Weather experts __________ how much water is in a cloud.

❹ Gamblers can never be __________ that their horse will win.

B Put the sentences in order.

❶ Weather forecasters predict when the cloud will reach a city.

❷ People decide whether to carry an umbrella.

❸ Weather forecasters look at how fast a cloud is moving.

❹ Weather forecasters predict the probability that rain will fall on the city.

__________ → __________ → __________ → __________

❶ Which of these is NOT a reason why data are used to present information?

   a) More information can be shown in a small space.

   b) People who speak different languages can understand the same data.

   c) It is impossible to show information using words.

   d) Presenting a graph is quicker and easier than writing information down.

❷ In which countries might you use these tally marks? Choose *two* answers.

   a) UK   b) France

   c) Spain   d) China

❸ Which of these do weather forecasters NOT use to predict the weather?

   a) rainfall data   b) temperature data

   c) wind speed data   d) full moon data

Let's Review the Story

Fill in the blanks to review the story.

Title: Fun __________ in Everyday Life

Chapter 1: Numbers

- The R ______ had their own numerals.
- The modern counting system is called the d ______ system.
- S ______ is often considered to be a lucky number.

Chapter 2: Measurement

- Roman measurements were taken from parts of the b ______ .
- The earliest clocks were s ______ .
- Julius ______ was the first person to divide the year into t ______ months.

Chapter 3: Shapes

- "Tessellation" means shapes that fit together without leaving g ______ .
- Many symmetrical patterns are found in n ______ .
- F ______ are patterns that repeat themselves as they get smaller and s ______ .

Chapter 4: Data

- Different countries use different t ______ marks, but each mark is usually a group of f ______ marks.
- The simplest kind of graph is the p ______ .
- P ______ can be used to forecast the weather.

Think about the following questions and answer them freely.

❶ Do you find math interesting or boring and difficult? Tell us what you think about math.

❷ In some cultures, there are some numbers that are considered to be lucky or unlucky. Which numbers symbolize good luck and which symbolize bad luck in different cultures? Why do they think those numbers symbolize good luck or bad luck? Organize some notes and tell us what you think.

❸ There are a lot of things that have symmetrical or fractal patterns in nature. Find more examples, organize some notes about them and tell us.

❹ Math exists everywhere in our everyday lives. Find examples of math that you meet in your everyday life other than the examples in the book and tell us about them.

Let's Review the Story

Title: Fun **Math** in Everyday Life

Chapter 1: Numbers

- The **Romans** had their own numerals.
- The modern counting system is called the **decimal** system.
- **Seven** is often considered to be a lucky number.

Chapter 2: Measurement

- Roman measurements were taken from parts of the **body**.
- The earliest clocks were **sundials**.
- Julius **Caesar** was the first person to divide the year into **twelve** months.

Chapter 3: Shapes

- "Tessellation" means shapes that fit together without leaving **gaps**.
- Many symmetrical patterns are found in **nature**.
- **Fractals** are patterns that repeat themselves as they get smaller and **smaller**.

Chapter 4: Data

- Different countries use different **tally** marks, but each mark is usually a group of **five** marks.
- The simplest kind of graph is the **pictograph**.
- **Probability** can be used to forecast the weather.

GOOD BEHAVIOR

After-reading Test

- Fun Math in Everyday Life
- Level 3
- 26 Questions

  (Vocabulary 5 / Reading Comprehension 16/

  Sentence Structure & Grammar 5)

1. Which of the following pair has the wrong past tense form of the verb?
   ① mean – meant
   ② shine – shone
   ③ hurt – hurt
   ④ choose – choosed

2. Which of the following pair has the wrong comparative form of the adjective?
   ① great – greater
   ② safe – safer
   ③ good – gooder
   ④ young – younger

3. Which of the following pair is NOT a pair of opposites?
   ① hard ↔ soft
   ② lucky ↔ gamble
   ③ upper ↔ lower
   ④ beginning ↔ end

4. Which of the following explains the meaning of "tessellation" the best?
   ① a method of making tiles for walls and floors
   ② a type of glue for fixing tiles to walls
   ③ a way in which shapes fit together without any gaps
   ④ a way in which objects are stored on shelves

5. What is the common word for the two blanks?

> • This is useful because our fingers and thumbs add up __________ ten.
> • In Chinese, the word for "four" sounds very similar __________ the word for "death."

① to
② of
③ on
④ with

6. Why was it a problem when there was no zero in early counting systems?
① It was difficult to count objects.
② It was difficult to perform calculations.
③ It was difficult to count backwards.
④ It was difficult to write down numerals.

7. In Italy, what does it mean "to do thirteen"?
① to win the grand prize
② to have a lot of bad luck
③ to have many children
④ to be close to death

8. According to the Bible, what does the number seven represent?
① bad luck
② completeness
③ nature
④ time passing

9. What problem did the Romans have in using parts of the body for measurements?

① Nobody knew which parts of the body to measure.
② Everyone's body had different measurements.
③ The Emperor did not tell anyone his measurements.
④ Different people used different parts of the body.

10. What were the earliest clocks?

① sundials   ② water clocks
③ candles   ④ hourglasses

11. In medieval times, where were mechanical clocks displayed?

① in people's homes   ② in town squares
③ in shops   ④ in churches

12. How many different constellations appeared in one year?

① six   ② ten
③ twelve   ④ twenty

13. Who first divided the year into twelve months?

① the Babylonians
② Julius Caesar
③ the queen of England
④ the king of France

14. Which of these shapes will NOT tessellate?

① rectangle

② square

③ triangle

④ circle

15. Why are circular tables useful?
① They fit better in rectangular rooms.
② More people can sit around them.
③ They fold away more easily than square tables.
④ They fit together without leaving any gaps.

16. Which of these is NOT symmetrical?
① a snowflake　　② a butterfly's wings
③ a fork of lightning　　④ a honeycomb cell

17. What is special about fractal patterns?
① They are symmetrical.
② They repeat themselves as they get smaller.
③ They fit together without leaving any gaps.
④ They are never found in nature.

18. Which of these is NOT an example of a fractal pattern?
① lightning   ② ferns
③ river valleys   ④ ladybug spots

19. In a tally, how many marks are there in each group?
① two   ② five
③ ten   ④ twenty

20. How is data shown in a pie chart?
① as bars   ② as lines
③ as pictures   ④ as pieces of a circle

21. How might parents use data when they are expecting a baby?
① to choose a name for the baby
② to find out whether the baby will be a boy or a girl
③ to predict how many children they will have
④ to discover when the baby will be born

※ Choose the wrong part of each sentence. (22~23)

22.
Some things are certain to not happen.
①   ②   ③   ④

23.
> There are <u>are</u> no corners <u>of</u> the food <u>to</u> <u>get</u> stuck in.
>   ①   ②   ③ ④

24. What is the correct word for the blank?

> People __________ speak different languages can understand
> the data.

① who   ② how

③ what   ④ which

※ Choose the correct sentence. (25~26)

25. ① Let's goes back to that question from Chapter 1 now.
   ② Let go back to that question for Chapter 1 now.
   ③ Now, let go back to that question from Chapter 1.
   ④ Now, let's go back to that question from Chapter 1.

26. ① They don't know what time do they wake up.
   ② They don't know what time wake up they.
   ③ They don't know what time they wake up.
   ④ They don't know what do they wake up time.

Sarah J. Dodd
Sarah J. Dodd is an experienced primary school teacher who resides in the UK, but has also lived and taught in Australia. She has a PhD in Science and a certificate in Creative Writing. She has published several books for children: "An Angel Anyway" (Anyway Press, 2008), the "Little Angels" series (Lion Children's Books, 2009/10), "The Lion Picture Bible" (Lion Children's Books, 2015) and "Legs: the tale of a meerkat lost and found" (Lion Children's Books, 2015). Her poetry for children has also been highly commended and published in the anthology "Let in the Stars" (Manchester Metropolitan University, 2014).
She is currently working on further picture books for the very young, and a novel for older children.

Fun Math in Everyday Life

Written by Sarah J. Dodd
Illustrated by Cheonso

First Published in August 2016

Editorial Manager: Juyon Choi
Editors: Kyunghee Jang, Jiyeong Park
Designer: Eunhee Lee
Cover Designer: Eunhee Lee

Published and distributed by

Darakwon Bldg., 64-1 Jandari-ro, Mapo-gu, Seoul, Korea 04031
Tel: 82-2-736-2031(ext. 250)   Fax: 82-2-732-2037
Homepage: www.ihappyhouse.co.kr
Publisher: Kyudo Chung

ISBN: 978-89-6653-410-4 18740 / 978-89-6653-156-1 18740(set)

[Components]
• 1 Audio CD (Recording Studio: Aram)
• Answer Keys & Korean Translation: Free download at www.ihappyhouse.co.kr